First published in the UK in 2018 by Studio Press Books,
an imprint of Kings Road Publishing,
part of Bonnier Books UK,
The Plaza, 535 King's Road,
London, SW10 0SZ

studiopressbooks.co.uk
bonnierbooks.co.uk

Printed in Italy, 0321018
1 3 5 7 9 10 8 6 4 2

ISBN 978-1-78741-357-3

Written by Emma Drage
Designed by Nia Williams
Illustrated by Maurizio Campidelli, Amy Zhing, Jenny Palmer and Kawaii Studio
Cover illustrated by Maurizio Campidelli

MICKEY IS MISSING!

Mickey and his friends have set off on an amazing globe-trotting adventure, exploring the wonders of Planet Earth and beyond! Can you track them down as they travel around the world? You'll need to be fast to keep up!

MICKEY

Playful and energetic, Mickey loves to have fun and always sees the humorous side of life! He's always positive, brave and resourceful. With Mickey, everything is more joyful, more adventurous and more magical!

MINNIE

Sweet and affectionate, but also determined and daring, Minnie is a free spirit who loves adventures.

DONALD

Unlucky Donald often loses his temper when things don't go according to plan, but he never gives up, especially when his family needs him!

DAISY

Charming and intelligent, Daisy might have a fiery temper at times, but she can also be incredibly generous and helpful, as long as she can do it in style.

PLUTO

Happy and playful, but rather clumsy, Pluto is Mickey's best friend and is always ready to play!

GOOFY

Sensitive Goofy is a loyal companion, but his trusting nature can sometimes lead him into danger. However, he will never say no to his friend Mickey when there is a new adventure coming up.

LOCATIONS

Look out for Mickey and friends as they travel through space and time! In each location, you'll find Mickey, Minnie, Donald, Daisy, Goofy and Pluto as they cross oceans, sail down rivers, explore mountains and cities, and even journey into space! Turn to the back for a list of more characters and objects to search for in the scenes.

MISSISSIPPI

ARGENTINA

SWITZERLAND

HAWAII

CHINA

EGYPT

4

GERMANY

DISNEYLAND

ROME

HOLLYWOOD

LONDON

PARIS

RIO DE JANEIRO

THE MOON

MISSISSIPPI

All aboard! Mickey and friends are embarking on an adventure down the Mississippi River. Can you spot them amongst the other steamboat passengers? Which of Mickey's friends is more interested in their own reflection than the view?

ARGENTINA

Mickey and friends have donned their dancing shoes for the tango! Can you find Mickey and Minnie amongst the couples hitting the dance floor? Which of Mickey's friends is losing his temper?

SWITZERLAND

It's picnic time in the Swiss mountains. Crowds have gathered to enjoy their lunch in the sunshine. The smell of food has attracted lots of four-legged friends to join in the fun. Can you spot Mickey's best friend, Pluto, amongst the crowd?

HAWAII

Welcome to the tropical beaches of Hawaii. As the sea sparkles in the sunshine and the gentle breeze blows through the palm trees, the band begins to play. Can you spot one of Mickey's friends enjoying a delicious ice cream?

CHINA

The Great Wall of China is packed with sightseers who have trekked from far and wide to admire the scenery. As fireworks light up the night sky, can you spot Mickey and friends amongst the other tourists?

15

EGYPT

Welcome to the land of the pyramids! Mickey and friends are embarking on a cruise down the Nile. Can you spot them amongst the passengers? Which of Mickey's friends is having their photograph taken on the riverbank?

GERMANY

In the shadow of an enormous medieval castle, Mickey and friends can be found amongst the crowd. Can you spot Minnie dressed as a princess? Who is taking a nap next to one of the guards?

DISNEYLAND

Welcome to Disneyland Paris!
You will see Mickey as the Sorcerer's
Apprentice watching the holidaymakers
as they stroll through the park, admiring
the fairy tale castle. Which of his friends
can you see enjoying a train ride?

ROME

Welcome to Rome, the eternal city!
Can you spot Mickey and friends among
the tourists admiring the sights of
Italy's capital? Whose nephews are
enjoying some local gelato? Look out
for Pluto taking a refreshing dip...!

HOLLYWOOD

As Mickey and Minnie take a bow on the red carpet in front of well-wishers and photographers, can you spot any familiar faces in the crowd? Which four-legged friend has come to keep them company?

LONDON

As ice and snow glisten on
London's rooftops, Mickey and friends are
preparing for a frosty holiday season in England.
Can you spot them joining in the festive fun?
Look out for some familiar faces
in the windows as well!

PARIS

The streets are packed as Minnie arrives in the French capital! While she travels in style in a horse-drawn carriage, can you spot Mickey and friends amongst the crowds gathered to welcome her to the city?

RIO DE JANEIRO

It's carnival time in Brazil!
The streets are filled with music and
dancing, and crowds gather to join the
festivities. Can you spot Mickey amongst
the partygoers? Which of his friends are
enjoying pride of place on the float?

THE MOON

After exploring the globe, Mickey travels through time and space to make his first appearance on the moon. Can you spot him amongst the intergalactic adventurers in this lunar city of the future?

MORE CHARACTERS AND OBJECTS TO SEARCH AND FIND

MISSISSIPPI
- Captain Pete
- Bar of soap
- Bucket of water
- Parrot
- Goat
- Cow

ARGENTINA
- Rhea (a bird)
- Wanted poster of El Gaucho
- Pete
- Swords
- Pot
- Fly in soup

SWITZERLAND
- Mickey's car
- Three picnic baskets
- Gramophone
- Dog's bone
- Dog's kennel
- Moose

HAWAII
- Paddy Pig
- Deep sea diver
- Bee
- Beach ball
- Tornado
- Turtle

CHINA
- Mother eagle
- Father eagle
- Bolivar the dog
- Lasso rope
- Nest with eggs
- Baby eagle

EGYPT
- Pot of paint
- Ship's wheel
- Anchor
- Flag with yellow stripe
- Band
- Grey cat

GERMANY
- Fly swat
- Poster of a giant
- Tailor's scissors
- King
- Baby in pram
- Horse head sign

DISNEYLAND
- Child with a red balloon
- Child with a little green flag
- Road clock
- Man holding an ice cream
- Man looking at a map
- Spell book

ROME
- Newspaper
- Mickey's red car
- Cow
- Huey, Dewey and Louie
- Trident
- Waiter carrying a silver cloche

HOLLYWOOD
- A reporter
- Bag of popcorn
- Movie ticket
- Clapper board
- Ice cream
- Photographer in a tree

LONDON
- Jiminy Cricket
- Willie the Giant
- Pete
- J. Thaddeus Toad
- Otto
- Three Little Pigs singing carols

PARIS
- Troubadour
- Beagle boys
- Six Royal Musketeers
- Bucket
- Pete
- Clarabelle

RIO DE JANEIRO
- Pete
- Horace Horsecollar
- Huey, Dewey, Louie
- Clarabelle

THE MOON
- Burger
- Five spaceships
- Ice cream
- Earth

ANSWERS

Mickey, Minnie, Donald, Daisy, Pluto and Goofy are circled in blue, and the other characters and objects to search and find are circled in red.

MISSISSIPPI

ARGENTINA

SWITZERLAND

HAWAII

CHINA

EGYPT

GERMANY

DISNEYLAND

ROME

HOLLYWOOD

LONDON

PARIS

RIO DE JANEIRO

THE MOON